Better Homes and Gardens®

DANDY DINOSAURS

Hi! My name is Max. I have some great projects to show you—and they're all about dinosaurs! We're going to have lots of fun making them together.

Inside You'll Find...

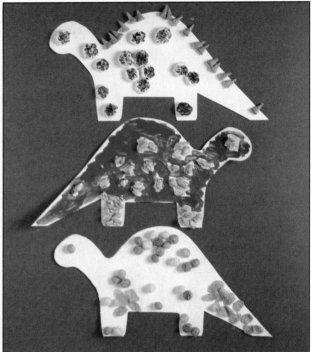

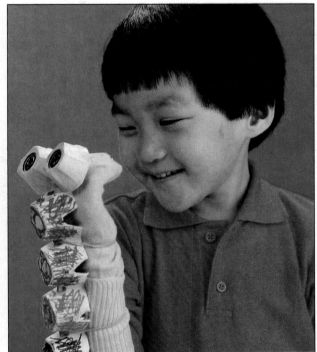

A celebration fit for a dinosaur.

Dinosaur Party!

Welcome to Max's party! Everyone is having lots of fun and laughing at these silly dinosaur riddles.

What time is it when a dinosaur sits on a fence?

Time to get a new fence!

What do you get when a dinosaur walks through a vegetable garden?

Squash.

What would happen if a dinosaur sat in front of you at a baseball game?

You would miss the game.

65TH MILLIONTH REUNION

Paper plates become an easy-to-make dinosaur headgear.

Stegosaurus Hat

A long, long time ago there was a dinosaur called a Stegosaurus. It had a big row of plates going down its back. Now you can look just like it when you make a Stegosaurus Hat.

What you'll need...

- 4 paper plates
- Crayons
- Stickers, ribbon, cotton balls, or yarn
- Stapler
- Pencil
- Two 24-inch pieces of yarn

1 Fold the paper plates in half. Draw designs on the plates any way you like and glue on stickers (see photo).

Lay 3 of the paper plates side by side lengthwise, overlapping about 1 inch. Make sure the folded edges make a straight line. Staple the 3 plates together where they overlap.

2 To make the headpiece, slide the last plate over one of the end plates (see photo).

The whole hat now looks like the number "7." Staple securely in place.

3 With adult help, use a pencil to punch a hole in each side of the headpiece plate. Insert 1 piece of yarn into each hole (see photo). Tie yarn in a knot to secure it in the hole. Tie the yarn under your chin to keep the hat on your head.

A simple dinosaur nose made from a cup.

Tyrannosaurus Rex Snouts

Grrrrr! Invite your friends over to your house for a growling snout-making party.

What you'll need...

- Scissors
- Plastic foam or paper cup with bottom removed
- Tape
- Four 2½-inch pieces of rickrack
- Super Snouts (see tip on page 9)
- Two 24-inch pieces of yarn

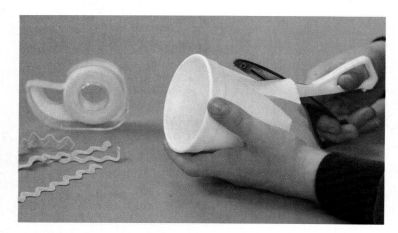

1 Starting at the bottom of the cup, cut 1 wedge out of the cup. This is 1 side of the mouth. Cut another wedge out of the cup, on the side opposite the first wedge (see photo).

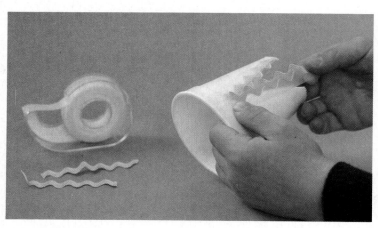

2 For the teeth, tape rickrack to the outer edges of the mouth (see photo). Decorate the snout any way you like (see Super Snouts tip).

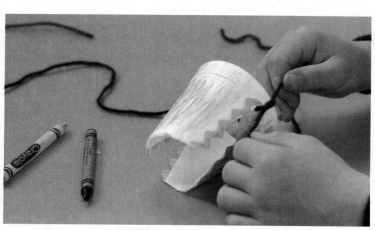

3 Tie a piece of yarn to each corner of the mouth (see photo). Put the snout up to your nose and tie the yarn around your head.

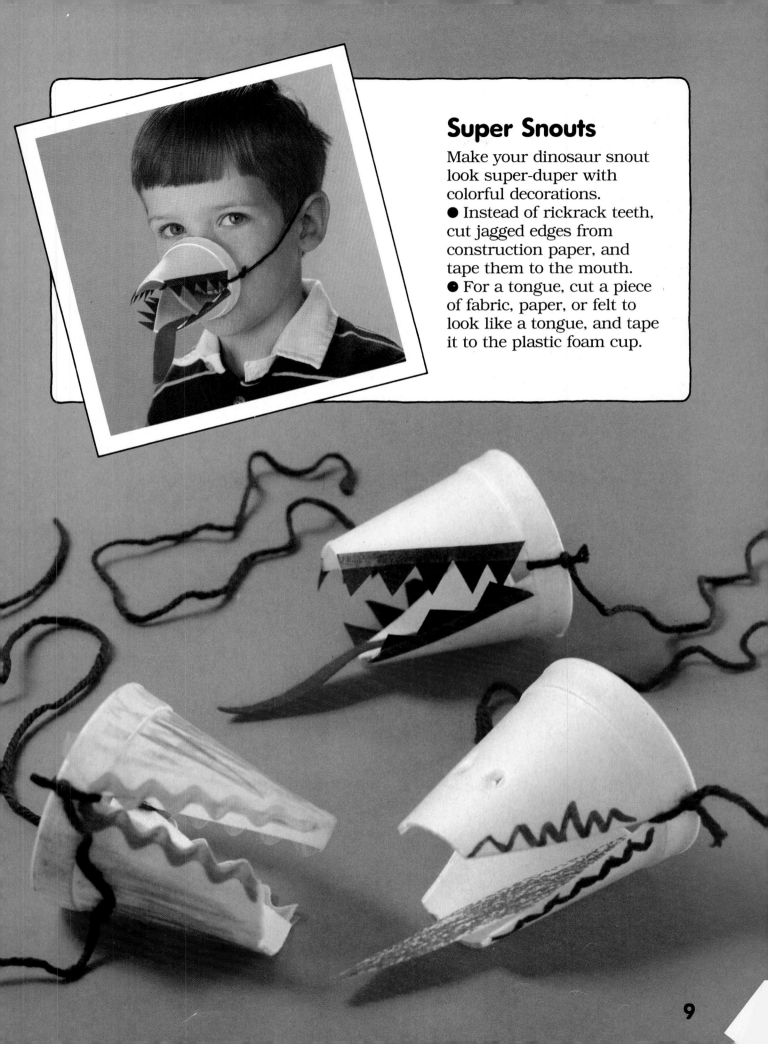

Super Snouts

Make your dinosaur snout look super-duper with colorful decorations.

● Instead of rickrack teeth, cut jagged edges from construction paper, and tape them to the mouth.

● For a tongue, cut a piece of fabric, paper, or felt to look like a tongue, and tape it to the plastic foam cup.

9

A beverage that those thirsty dinosaurs at your house can make.

Triceratops Sippers

How many horns does a Triceratops have? It has 3! And there are 3 delicious flavors in this fizzy ice cream drink.

What you'll need...

- Ice cream scoop
- Vanilla ice cream, softened
- Tall glass
- Orange or grape juice, or cranberry juice cocktail
- Lemon-lime carbonated beverage
- Stirrer or long-handled spoon
- Straws

1 For each drink, place a scoop of ice cream in a tall glass.

2 Fill each glass ¾ full with juice. Pour in enough lemon-lime beverage to fill the glass (see photo).

3 Stir the ice cream and liquid a few times (see photo). Add a straw to each drink.

Party Food For Kids

Don't stop with the Triceratops Sippers at your dinosaur party. Let everyone pitch in and make Munch a Bunch of Dinosaurs on page 16. Or, toss together a snack mix with popcorn, cereal, peanuts, and candy-coated milk chocolate pieces.

A clever maze filled with fascinating dinosaur information.

Amazing Dinosaurs

Oops! Where's Elliot and the picnic lunch? Help Max find the path to Elliot. Make sure that Max stops and visits the dinosaurs along the way.

 The Triceratops (try-SAIR-uh-tops) is also called "three-horned face." That's because it had 1 thick nose horn and 1 big horn above each eye. That makes a total of 3 horns.

The Ankylosaurus (ang-KILE-uh-sawr-us) is called "armored lizard." It had short, thick legs so it couldn't move very fast. Sometimes it used the end of its bony tail as a weapon.

The Brachiosaurus (BRAK-ee-uh-sawr-us), biggest of all the dinosaurs, spent lots of time in the water. Do you know why? Because that made it safe from other dinosaurs that couldn't swim.

One of the fiercest and greatest hunters ever was the Tyrannosaurus (tye-RAN-uh-sawr-us) rex. It's also called "king tyrant lizard" and ate other dinosaurs for food.

The Stegosaurus (STEG-uh-sawr-us) is called the "plated lizard" because it had a row of large bony plates that ran down its back and tail. Its brain was only the size of a walnut.

TAR PIT

Transform breakfast food into prehistoric animals.

Cereal Apatosaurus

Cereal isn't just for breakfast. Glue it onto a paper dinosaur to make a silly-looking creature with bumps and lumps.

What you'll need...

- Pencil
- Poster board or lightweight cardboard
- Scissors
- White crafts glue
- Dry cereal
- Tempera paint
- Waxed paper or newspapers
- Cotton swab or paintbrush

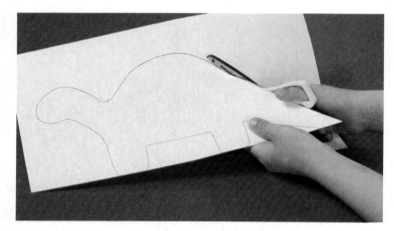

1 Using the dinosaurs on the opposite page as a guide, draw a dinosaur on the poster board. Cut the dinosaur out of the poster board (see photo).

2 Dab a small amount of glue onto the dinosaur. Place cereal on the glue. Repeat gluing and adding cereal until you have as much cereal on the dinosaur as you like (see photo). Let glue dry for a few hours or overnight.

3 If you like, paint your dinosaur. Cover your work surface with waxed paper. Use a cotton swab as a paintbrush (see photo). Let paint dry.

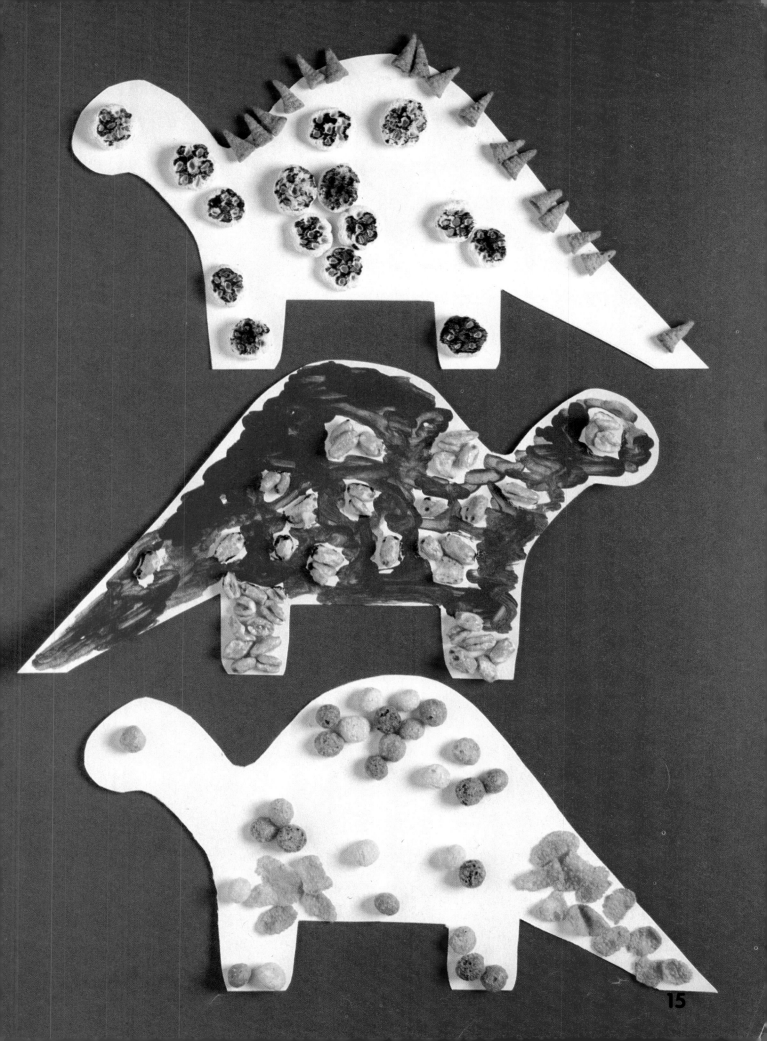

Your children create and then eat their very own dinosaurs.

Munch a Bunch of Dinosaurs

It's fun to shape this colorful cookie dough into prehistoric creatures. Then comes the best part—munching them!

What you'll need...

- Tape
- Waxed paper
- Dinosaur Dough (see page 31)
- Liquid or paste food coloring
- Foil
- Cookie sheet
- Hot pads
- Pancake turner
- Wire cooling rack

1 Tape pieces of waxed paper to the counter. You'll need one piece of waxed paper for each color. Divide cookie dough into several parts and place onto the pieces of waxed paper.

Add food coloring to each part. Squeeze the coloring into dough with your hands (see photo). Keep squeezing till the dough is all the same color.

2 Tear a piece of foil the size of your cookie sheet. Tape foil to the counter. Place a handful of cookie dough onto the foil. Shape cookies into dinosaurs or other shapes on the foil (see photo). Make sure the cookies are about ½ inch thick and about 2 inches apart on the foil.

3 Remove the tape from the foil. With adult help. carefully lift the foil and dough onto the cookie sheet.

With adult help, bake cookies in a 300° oven for 20 to 25 minutes or till the dough is set (edges are firm).

Use hot pads to remove the cookie sheet from the oven. With a pancake turner, lift the hot cookies off the foil and onto a wire rack. Let the cookies cool.

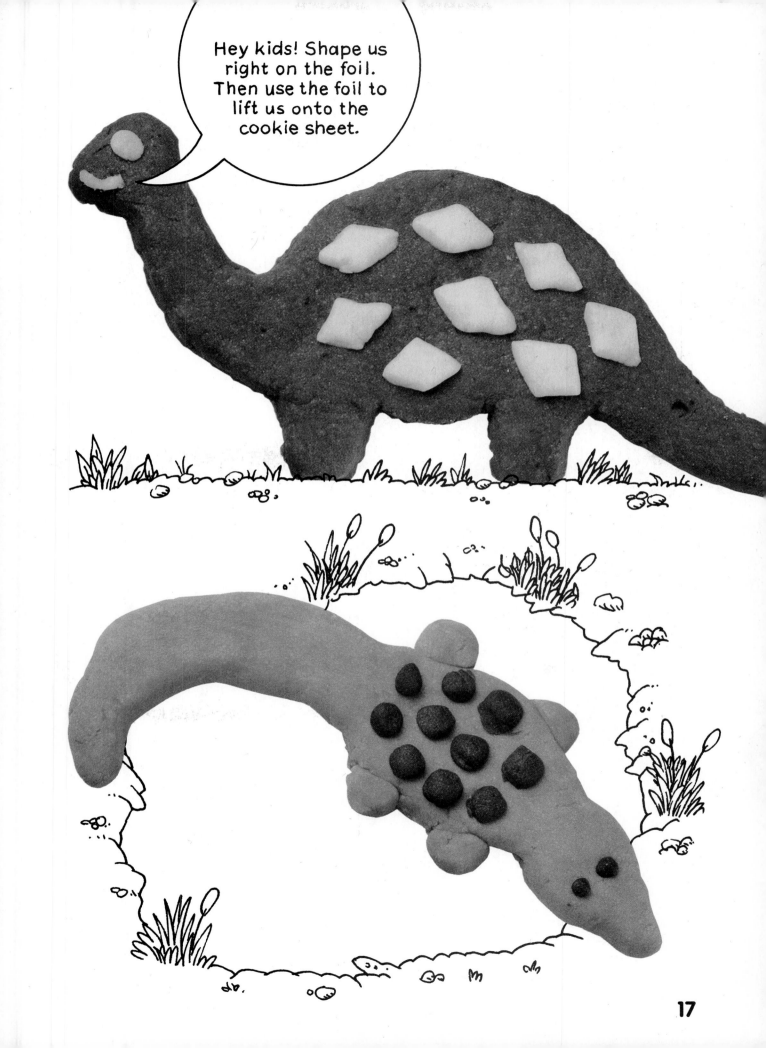

17

Baby Dinosaurs

Look! A little dinosaur just hatched out of its egg. Can you point to the 5 baby dinosaurs that are hiding in the jungle picture?

Did you know...

● Just like chickens, most dinosaurs laid eggs. But some dinosaur eggs were as big as 10 chicken eggs.

● The Apatosaurus (ah-PAT-uh-sawr-us), also known as the Brontosaurus (BRON-tuh-sawr-us), laid eggs that were 4 feet long—that's just about as big as you!

● There are lots of dinosaur footprints all over the world. Some places even have parks where you can look at dinosaur footprints.

● Dinosaur footprints help us learn more about dinosaurs. They can tell us where a dinosaur walked and lived.

Plain hard-cooked eggs become colorful dinosaur eggs.

Delicious Dinosaur Eggs

Make believe that you're an explorer who studies dinosaur eggs by eating them. You can make them right at home.

What you'll need...

- 4 hard-cooked eggs
- Small bowl
- 3 cups cool water

- 1 envelope unsweetened soft drink mix (choose bright colored mix)

- Clear plastic wrap

1 Gently tap the hard-cooked eggs all over till the shells crack (see photo). Do not take the shells off the eggs.

2 In a small bowl stir together water and soft drink mix. Add cracked eggs to the colored water (see photo).

3 Cover the small bowl with plastic wrap. Place it in the refrigerator. Leave the eggs in the bowl for 1 to 2 days. Remove the eggs and throw away the colored water. Peel the shells off the eggs (see photo). Your dinosaur eggs are ready to eat.

"Egg-citement!"

One of our kid-testers wasn't sure he wanted to taste a dinosaur egg. He thought our eggs were really pretty—"But do they taste as good as they look?" he asked. Once he bit into one, he could tell it was made with grape soft drink mix. "I like it! Can I make them?" he exclaimed.

Small handprints make wonderfully unique dinosaur prints.

Little Dinosaur Footprints

Pretend a baby dinosaur hatched in your house and left its footprints behind on a piece of paper. Where do the tracks go?

What you'll need...

- Newspaper or brown kraft paper
- Paper towel
- Water
- Plastic foam meat tray or small plate
- Paper
- Tempera paints

1 Cover your work surface with newspaper. Fold a paper towel so it will fit into the meat tray. Dampen paper towel with water and place it in meat tray. Pour a small amount of paint over paper towel. Make a fist and dip the side of your hand into the paint (see photo).

2 Press the painted part of your hand onto the paper. Lift your hand from the paper to see what kind of dinosaur footprint you made (see photo).

3 If you like, dip your thumb or fingers into the paint and add toes or claws to the footprint (see photo). Let the paint dry.

Don't forget to wash your hands!

Stretch out the fingers on your hand. Dip only 2 of your fingers into the paint. Make a print.

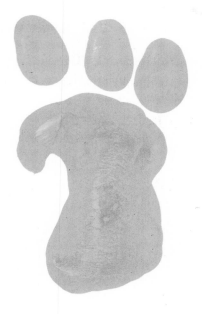

Make your hand into a tight fist. Dip the side of your hand into the paint. Make a print. Lift hand and make 2 more prints.

Make a fist and dip the side of your hand into the paint. Make a print while rolling your hand back and forth. Dip your thumb into the paint. Make 3 thumbprints for the toes.

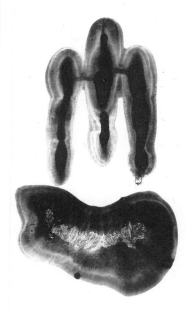

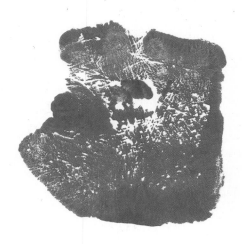

Stretch out the fingers on your hand. Dip only 3 of your fingers into the paint. Make a print. Dip your palm into the paint. Make a print.

Make your hand into a tight fist. Dip the side of your hand into the paint. Make a print onto paper. Dip the tip of a finger into paint. Make 2 fingerprints for toes.

Stretch out fingers on your hand. Try to keep all of your fingers out of the paint. Dip only your palm into the paint. Make a print.

23

A prehistoric playground that helps children recognize opposites.

Playful Dinosaurs

Max and his friends are playing, giggling, and having a great time. What do you like to do when you're at the playground?

Look at the dinosaurs playing on the teeter-totter.
Which one is going up?
Which one is going down?

Look at the dinosaurs playing catch.
Which one is near?
Which one is far?

Look at Max and Elliot.
Who is inside the playhouse?
Who is outside the playhouse?

An ordinary sock becomes an extraordinary dinosaur puppet.

Prehistoric Puppet

What's better than a talking puppet? A talking puppet that looks like a dinosaur! Can you make your puppet talk?

What you'll need...

- Markers or crayons
- 1 strip of 4 paper egg carton cups, attached
- 1 strip of 2 paper egg carton cups, attached
- 1 sock
- 2 rubber bands
- Tape

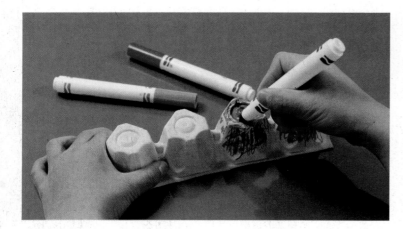

1 Use markers to decorate the 4 egg cups any way you like (see tip on page 27). Draw eyes on the 2 egg cups.

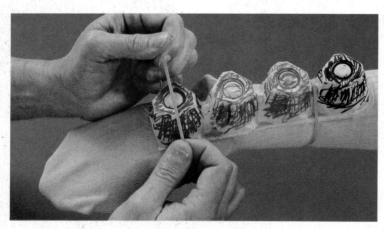

2 Slip your hand inside the sock. Place the 4 egg cups on top of the sock. With adult help, put a rubber band on each end of the cups (see photo). The rubber bands help keep the egg cups on your arm.

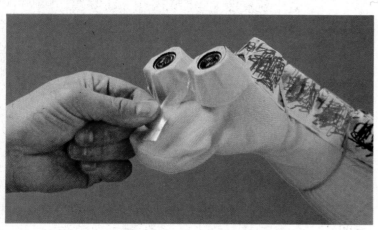

3 With adult help, tape the eyes to the sock near the toe (see photo). Now open and close your hand to make your puppet look like it's talking.

Pretty Egg Cups

Decorate your dinosaur puppet any way you like.

● Use markers, crayons, or colored pencils to color right on the 4 egg cups.

● Dab glue on the egg cups and sprinkle with glitter.

● Paint each egg cup a different color.

What other ways could you decorate your puppet?

An amusing finger rhyme about dinosaurs.

Crazy Dinosaurs

Wiggle and stretch your 5 fingers! Now you're ready to use them as you listen to this funny dinosaur poem.

Five crazy dinosaurs
cleaning up the floor.
One got swept away
and then there were four.

Four crazy dinosaurs
chased by a bee.
One got stung
and then there were three.

Three crazy dinosaurs
playing with some glue.
One got stuck
and then there were two.

Two crazy dinosaurs
out for a run.
One fell down
and then there was one.

One crazy dinosaur,
acting like a hero,
went to save the others
and then there were zero.

5

4

3

2

1

Parents' Pages

We've filled this special section with more activities, recipes, reading suggestions, hints we learned from our kid-testers, and many other helpful tips.

Dinosaur Party!

See pages 4 and 5

A little rusty at planning a children's party? Then here are some answers.

● *How should I invite people?*
By phone *or* by mail. If you have the time, you and your children could make simple dinosaur invitations. Include the date, beginning and ending times, address, phone number, and R.S.V.P. request.

● *When's the best time?*
Try scheduling a time when the kids will be at their best. For preschool kids, it's important that the party doesn't interfere with their naps. And school-age children may be too tired from the day's activities to attend an after-school party.

● *How long should it last?*
Limit the party to about 1 hour for 4- to 6-year-olds and about 2 hours for older children.

Stegosaurus Hat

See pages 6 and 7

You can make the hat as long as you and your children like. It's easy to add on more plates. Just fold and decorate additional plates and staple them to the end of the tail. Tell your children that dragons also have long tails. Ask them to make believe they're dragons and then have them pretend to be dinosaurs. Are their actions the same or different?

You might also want to show your children how to add some "spikes" to the ends of their hats. On one of the folded plates, draw a line about ½ inch above the fold. Using this as the baseline, draw two or three triangles side by side on the plate with the points at the rounded edge. Cut through the plate along the sides of the triangles, being careful not to cut through the baseline. Decorate this plate and then staple it onto the end of the hat.

Spikes for Stegosaurus hat

Tyrannosaurus Rex Snouts

See pages 8 and 9

Tyrannosaurus rex was one of the fiercest dinosaurs. So our kid-testers thought this project's name was just right.

For an easy-to-make Halloween costume, couple a snout with the Stegosaurus Party Hat. Apply green face paint (available at theatrical shops) to your Halloweener's face and hands for a dinosaur touch.

Triceratops Sippers

See pages 10 and 11

For a simple backyard party game, write numbers on small pieces of paper. Tape them to the bottoms of the glasses before filling with the beverage.

When your little guests are done with their drinks, have them turn the glasses over to look at their numbers. By doing this outdoors, spilling the drink drippings won't matter.

Give each child an inexpensive gift with a number on it that matches the number taped to his or her glass.

Amazing Dinosaurs

See pages 12 and 13

Your children may already know how to pronounce the names of the dinosaurs in this maze. If they do, have them "teach" you how to say STEG-uh-sawr-us and the others. Most kids enjoy getting a chance to be the teacher. If they haven't learned the names yet, practice the pronunciations together.
● Reading suggestions:
Dinosaurs
   by Gail Gibbons
Dinosaur Bones
   by Aliki
What Happened to Patrick's Dinosaurs?
   by Carol Carrick

Cereal Apatosaurus

See pages 14 and 15

Once your children have made cereal dinosaurs, ask them if they would like to make a Christmas tree for the holidays. Your children can cut a tree out of construction paper and glue on cereal for lights. They could put cereal under the tree for presents.

Giving Cookies

Baking cookies is twice the fun when you share the results with someone. Whether it's a special holiday, a birthday, welcoming a new neighbor, saying thank you to someone, or cheering up a friend, a batch of home-baked cookies brightens the day for both of you.

Present the cookies in a gaily wrapped shoe box, a decorated coffee can, or a wide-mouthed jar you label "Cookie Jar."

Munch a Bunch Of Dinosaurs

See pages 16 and 17

To avoid spills or excess color, you may prefer to add the food coloring to the dough yourself. Just knead the color in slightly, then let the child squeeze the dough until the color's evenly mixed.

Dinosaur Dough

  ⅔ cup margarine
     or butter
1⅔ cups all-purpose flour
  ⅓ cup sugar
  ½ teaspoon vanilla
     or almond extract

● In a large mixer bowl beat the margarine with an electric mixer on medium speed about 30 seconds or till softened.
● Add about half of the flour, the sugar, and the vanilla.
● Beat with an electric mixer on low to medium speed till thoroughly combined, scraping the sides of the bowl occasionally.
● Then beat or stir in the remaining flour.
● Shape and bake cookies as directed on page 16.
● Makes about 10 big cookies.

Baby Dinosaurs

See pages 18 and 19

Your children won't find baby dinosaur footprints in their backyard, but they can look for tracks left by other nighttime visitors.

On a still night, dust a small area of the ground with flour or baby powder. Leave a scrap of food such as bread or cheese in the middle of the dusted area. The next morning, go outside and look for footprints. Try to guess what animal or animals had a midnight snack and left their tracks.
● Reading suggestion:
Baby Dinosaurs
   by Helen Roney Sattler

Delicious Dinosaur Eggs

See pages 20 and 21

The key to making pretty marbled eggs is during the first step. Crack the shells gently so you'll get lots of fine cracks.

If you crack the shells too hard, they will split open. Then, the soft drink mix will seep inside the shell and leave big blotches of color on the egg instead of a delicate marbling.

(continued from page 31)

These Delicious Dinosaur Eggs also can double as beautiful Easter eggs. After your children peel the marbled eggs, wrap in clear plastic wrap. Then tie the ends with a colorful piece of ribbon.

Place them in an Easter basket for a colorful springtime treat. Be sure to store the eggs in the refrigerator.
● Reading suggestion:
The Dinosaur Eggs
    by Francis Mosley

Little Dinosaur Footprints

See pages 22 and 23

Let your children make their footprints. Go outside and have them paint the bottoms of their feet with tempera paint. Have them walk around on a large piece of white paper. When the footprinted paper dries, use it for wrapping paper. Grandparents will love it!

Playful Dinosaurs

See pages 24 and 25

Looking at these dinosaurs having fun at a playground is a great way to show your children opposites. You also can have your children find other opposites in the book. For example, on pages 12 and 13, have them look at the dinosaur path. There is a start and a finish for the path; sometimes the path curves up and sometimes it curves down.

To reinforce the concept of opposites, have your children look through old magazines and cut out pictures of opposites. For example, look for something hot and cold, or big and little. Then paste the opposites side by side onto paper. Staple the pages together to make a scrapbook.
● Reading suggestions:
How Big Is a Brachiosaurus?
    by Susan Carroll
The Missing Dinosaur Bone
    by Stan and Jan
    Berenstain

Prehistoric Puppet

See pages 26 and 27

It's easy to make a "stage" so your kids can have a dinosaur puppet show. Just follow these steps:
● To make the puppet stage, find a small cardboard box.

Cut half of the bottom panel out of the box. If you have a deep box, trim the sides so they are about 3 inches wide.
● Let your children decorate the box any way they like.
● Stand the box up on the end of a table. Be sure the cutout is on top (see photo).
● Now, have your children squat down behind the box and bring their puppets up through the opening.
● Now sit back and enjoy the show!

Crazy Dinosaurs

See pages 28 and 29

The first few times you read this funny counting rhyme to your children, show them how to hold their fingers and count along. Once they can follow that easily, encourage them to recite the rhyme along with you. Before long, they'll be able to teach this simple rhyme to all their friends.
● Reading suggestion:
Dinosaurs
    Poems selected by
    Lee Bennett Hopkins

BETTER HOMES AND GARDENS® BOOKS
Editor: Gerald M. Knox
Art Director: Ernest Shelton
Managing Editor: David A. Kirchner
Department Head, Food and Family Life: Sharyl Heiken

DANDY DINOSAURS
Editors: Sandra Granseth and Linda Foley Woodrum
Editorial Project Manager: Liz Anderson
Graphic Designers: Harijs Priekulis and Linda Ford Vermie
Contributing Illustrator: Buck Jones
Contributing Photographer: Perry Struse

Have BETTER HOMES AND GARDENS®
magazine delivered to your door.
For information, write to:
ROBERT AUSTIN
P.O. BOX 4536
DES MOINES, IA. 50336